POEMS BY
MOIRA ANDREW

LIGHT
THE
BLUE
TOUCH
PAPER

IRON PRESS

For Fiona and Jennifer

© Copyright 1986 Moira Andrew

First Published 1986 by IRON Press
5 Marden Terrace, Cullercoats
North Shields, Tyne & Wear NE30 4PD
Tel: Tyneside (091) 2531901

Second Edition 1989.

Printed by Tyneside Free Press Workshop
5 Charlotte Square, Newcastle upon Tyne

Typeset by True North in 10pt Sabon Medium

Cover Design by Norman Leater

ISBN 0906228 28 X

19/2/97

IRON Press books distributed by;
Password Books Ltd,
25 Horsell Rd, London N1 1XL
Tel: 01-607-1154

WITH THE ASSISTANCE OF

SOUTH WEST ARTS

Book paste-up by Norman Davison

MOIRA ANDREW was born and educated in Scotland. She is a former primary head teacher and College of Education lecturer. Now living in Wales, Moira is a full-time freelance writer and poet-in-schools. She has published three collections of poems. For children she has edited several anthologies, all from Macmillan Education. Her most recent book is one for teachers, LANGUAGE IN COLOUR, published by Belair Publications Ltd., 1989. Moira Andrew's own poems for children appear in a number of anthologies.

Acknowledgements:

Some of these poems have appeared in South West Review, 'A Celebration' (SW Arts), Outposts, Iron, the Iron Press anthology, Orbis, Arts Council Anthology 8, The Countryman, 'Invisible Lipstick' (Stone Edge Press, 1985) and Macmillan anthologies for juniors. Several have also been published in Priapus Press booklets, 'The Swing Park', (1983) and 'Broken Morning', (1985). 'The Swing Park' won the Open University competition in 1982.

CONTENTS

Light the blue touch paper

Owls shred the night
into ribbons.
Second-hand music
brushes past
the cornerstone.

Experimentally
you touch my cheek.
'Kiss you?' smudges
the air
between us.

Your hands
are full of promise,
fingers
wired for sex.
I lean close.

We are negatives
of our daylight selves,
charged,
pulsed to shed
our wrappings.

'Make love?'
a ghosted question
in the cool instant
before the current
surges.

We are fused
into a single substance,
you, me, the owl-dark trees,
and borrowed music
bonds us.

The swing park

We lie close enough
for me to hear
your eyes open.
'Remember . . . remember
that first night?
You wore a white
tight-belted coat?'

I'd forgotten that coat.

We sat on high stools,
I remember, camouflaged
by a pall of small-talk.
Then we escaped, biting
into the night, crisp
as a Hallowe'en apple.
'Where to?' you said.

Not that it mattered.

We came to the park.
Our gloved hands
stirred the swings
hanging cold in chains.
'Children under 14 only'
Ghosted metronomes,
we swung on borrowed time.

But nobody cared.

Breathing dragon smoke
we laughed, voices clanging
in the empty bucket
of the night. We were hushed.
The weir tumbled greedily
into the quiet of frost.
You pocketed my hand.

And that's how it was.

We lie in jigsaw pieces
talking and not talking.
'Remember swinging like kids?'
'You nearly froze to death,
I remember. Nothing's changed.'
And the years between
might not have been.

My feet were always cold.

Rosie

She came from her mother
easily, without the pain
that Emma brought. She came
with a smile for the world.
'Too good to be true,'
the father said, marvelling.

She suckled intuitively,
milky as a piglet, eyes
meandering. Her mother's face
dissolved into a globe
of nourishment. Cherishing her,
they called her Rosie Jane.

'Not half the trouble
Emma was,' they said.
She slept deeply, snug
as a hot water bottle,
all night long. Her days
were placid, undemanding.

'Such a happy baby' – yet
they worried. She didn't cry.
'Not quite perfect,' doctors said.
Trusting, not comprehending tears,
Rosie laughed, a bruised plum
in the bottom of the basket.

Bath-time
(For David)

every morning
I read poetry
in the bath

like ripe grapes
words hang heavy
on the page

my eyes harvest
ideas, my mind
drinks deep

images bubble up
or wait vat-dark
for maturity

in the evening
the baby sits
squat as a frog

his skin glistening,
his small sex
an underwater weed

he sucks, splashes
squeezes, dribbles
and poems

flow through him,
intoxicating
without words

Two in May

The child wakes, stretches,
still frothy with sleep,
like a cherry tree all fat
with blossom. His eyes
are bluebells, deep and
bright as flowers found
in a hollow, untroubled
by the secrets of living.
He reaches out for me,
and his words tumble
over one another, thick
and quick and green as
leaves unfolding in May.

Still life

The day is deadlocked by heat.
Doors stand open all along
the street and telephones
are silent.
        A baby cries
in a thin half-hearted way
too hot to feed, too sweated
for sleep. Lawn mowers idle
in empty gardens; sprinklers
mizzle to themselves in great
pinwheels on the grass.
Washing hangs dead-crow limp
and flowers faint.
            I swing
slow circles of lettuce
in its wire basket, water
piddling warm over bare feet.

Pooled resources

'Swim me gold,'
sobs the fish.
'Sway me deep,'
spirals tethered weed.

'Float me tender
on the water's skin.'
And the lily
sails majestic, holding
cupped hands
to the sun.

Summer smalltalk

It was the sundress
that did it –
a strappy shoestring
affair.

'Flimsy,'
said the gardener.
'Like a gardenia
petal.'

'Exciting,'
said the artist.
'Emphasises body
line.'

'Nice,'
said the lover.
'Let's have it
off.'

High summer

The sun
burns a hole
in the trees,
stretches quietness
to breaking
point.

Sweat
salts our eyes
and a curdled light
weighs down the
stoodstill after-
noon.

Beneath
bruised tassels
a buddleia droops
purpling. And never
a bird or a
breath.

Butterflies
freewheel down
the air, pitch brown
tents, pale thumbprints
on buddleia
boughs.

'Fifty?'
'Nearer sixty –'
Impossible to count,
they cluster in drab
prologue waiting.
On cue

they open
wide-eyed backs
to the sun. We watch,
keep the thought of them;
pop-up cards for
Christmas.

Love in the afternoon

I wore my new blue dress for you.
I smiled to welcome you
and made you coffee. You fingered
my dress and said how does it undo?
and thank you for the coffee.
I mustn't wait. Remember,
I have a wife at home.

The coffee was too hot to drink.
You sat beside me and the first kiss
was gentle, dry. I just dropped by
to bring these books. No I didn't.
I came to see you, you said,
fingers sliding down the slopes
of me. My wife, you said, remembering.

You unbuttoned my new dress, and
breasts spilled into your hands.
You explored my face, tracing
each shape with teeth and tongue.
You crushed my new blue dress
and in brown matching mugs
the coffee cooled.

You threw my blue dress on the floor
beside the abandoned knock-kneed mugs
and said I love you. I love you too I said.
I touched the foxglove pride of you
and in the quiet of afternoon
our bodies sang in tune. You watched me
dress. I'll make fresh coffee, I said.

Morning after

The open door
lets morning in
and the cool smell
of summer flows
to meet dark rhythms
of percolating coffee.

Sunshine is echoed
in fringed marigolds
on the window sill,
lingers in marmalade
on breakfast toast
and magnifies the dust.

They eat in silence.

Night is pocketed
carefully behind
their eyes. Ravelled
tights and socks
and underthings
are cleared away.

They wash up
breakfast dishes
and glasses puddled
with last night's wine.
Smiling secretly, they
turn from the sun.

'I'll be in touch.'

He kisses her, dry
as a friendly uncle
and drives away
without looking back.
She should smooth out
the creases of darkness

but
opens the 'Sunday Times'
instead.

Impression of love

You fill my head with love-speak
pour my body like hot wax from
the complacency of clothes

You leave identification tags
on my skin, tattooing bite marks
where they won't show

You print your bone-shapes along
my bones, set your seal on me
in shuddering seed

Future imperfect

I remember
when I had
rounded elbows

and tomorrows
stretched yellow
beyond the walls

of our house
like a line
of washing

blowing in the sun

I dreamed of
adulthood when
books would voice

their wisdom
without brainscrews
of effort

on my part
I anticipated
adding my words

to those already in print

I used to wear
spotted dresses
(Shirley Temple style)

but hankered after
long-skirted frocks
like those

my mother had
for evenings
when she smelled different

and even buffed her nails

I wondered
what being grown-up
was like

I could have
told you
It's loving

& dying
pretending & spending
screwing & screaming & daydreaming

all in a skin that doesn't fit
anymore

Out in the real world

I found a jewel
in the long grass
its eye blinking
under the sun.

Just a dewdrop,
mother said.
Come inside before
your shoes get wet.

I heard reindeer bells
above the roof, an
empty glass and biscuit
crumbs were proof.

Your dad dressed up,
they scoffed at school.
Everyone in the world
knows that.

Woman now, I made
a home, ironed shirts,
baked tarts, loved
through all the dark.

But — just a house,
a base, he said,
a place to sleep
most nights.

'Ice to suck'

(In Glasgow's Victoria Infirmary the progress of post-operative patients is charted according to a printed notice by the bed-side: 'Nil by mouth', 'Ice to suck', 'Fluids only')

She used to suck peppermints,
loved Aunt Nannie's home-made
tablet and Bournville chocolate.
She kept a supply of sweets
in wrinkled paper bags.

Breakfast was her favourite
meal; porridge, bacon and egg
and toast. Thin as a cucumber
sandwich she drowses, nourished
now, drop by Dextrose drop.

White hair fans white pillow,
a plastic bracelet gives
her name; only eyes and rings
Telex true identity. The ward
smells cabbage-water sweet.

Trapped in time remembered
she frets; lopsided tongue
lolls from old baby mouth.
We offer a gauze-wrapped cube,
comfort her with ice to suck.

Letter home

She was never to be parted
from her handbag, you know
the way children are. Blue,
it was, geriatric, with a
cobbled handle, and the fuss,
tears, if it went missing!

Sometimes I grubbed around
inside, finding Smarties,
sticky chocolate buttons,
some ten pence pieces and
broken beads. The letter
was on a scrap of paper,

the writing immature, un-
formed. 'Dear Mum & Dad,
Just a quick note to let
you know I arrived here
yesterday afternoon. The
house is very large and

has umpteen bedrooms, some
made out of one big room.
I have one of these. All
the guests are fairly
ancient, like me. see
you soon. Love, Dolly.'

They fed her from a spoon,
tucked her up at night,
a child in a frilled gown,
the letter home unstamped,
unposted. The bag is jumble,
the message haunts me still.

Broken morning

A blackbird
scrapes
the lightening sky
with knives of song,
wounds emptiness
with the lacerations
of its first
bleak notes.

The blackbird
sharpens
nightlong coldness
on a strop of frost,
whets loneliness
with its pale music
and I half-hear
a remembered voice.

Another year, another spring

It might have been
the first time, new
morning watching for
the sun, fields grey
in a shiver of light,
an opening door
and that voice
from the woods,
cruel
    clear
        cuckoo

I cup springtime
in my two hands, hold
back the climbing day,
halt primroses and
scattered celandines
with a click of
the latch. The cuckoo
picks the lock,
follows
    me
       indoors

Maentwrog in the morning

The sky leans elbows
on the hills, rests its
head among the clouds.
Trees crowd the slopes,
curl close as a collar,
and the river unreels
silver threads along
the valley. The village
wears its houses like
worry beads, slate-grey
with constant fingering.

The Queen

In the web-grey light
of early dawn, before
the public pomp of spilled
champagne and celebration,
we drove in secret
to greet the Queen. 'Last
of her line,' said Jack.

Cranes, like long-necked
prehistoric birds
laddered the skyline.
Single hammer strokes sang
inside her echoing hull.
Jacked up on stilts
she waited for her name.

'Proud day,' Jack said.
'Sad too. They'll never
build her like again.'
Reluctant to turn away
his cold hand grazed
my cheek. 'You won't
forget this morning?'

When the QE2 returned
from war, rusted,
pennanted in Union flags
and tears, I remembered;
'Launched into history,'
he'd said, still lingering.
Breakfast didn't matter.

Escape tactics

clock licks darkness
with a green tongue

clothes make molehills
on the floor

lovers tunnel through
the yielding hours

before daylight
and blind telephones

spring the gin-trap
of loneliness

Under cover of darkness

Late in the evening
after the wine and the coffee
and the cake, my coat on
and zipped up, you said
I'm not used to being alone.
Will you spend the night
with me?

I considered lights on
at home and the neighbours
and not having a toothbrush
and thought What the hell?
You looked screwed up, victim
of throwaway society. I said
I'd stay.

You ran a bath, tipped in
foam. I scrubbed your back.
Salvaged, we Mark 2 lovers
keyed into the safe dark.
Thanks, you said. I wrote
this poem in my head and said
See you.

Yesterday's fable

("Persuasion is better than force" – Aesop)

He breezes into her life,
buys drinks, a meal –
a ticket to her bed.

She fends him off with
coffee, conversation.
Delay clouds his patience.

He tires of playing games,
tries storm tactics
attacking lips and zips

making flotsam of her finery.
She resists his force eight
frenzy, abruptly yields

lying half-clothed, passive.
He storms out, confused
as an occluded front.

She shelters in tatters
of dress and dignity
forecasting the police

all gaping notebooks
inflexible eyes, How long
have you known this Mr North?

She meets Solly at a party,
basks in bright intervals
of flattery, warms to him.

His fingers gentle her.
Clothes fall like petals
in the heat of summer.

A day in the life of a poet

You meet a man one morning
and ask him to read poems
with you. I don't know, he says.
I'm not much good at poetry,
but he agrees. He reads
a Brian Patten love poem
and one by Wes Magee.
You choose 'Poem in October'
and two of your own.

You walk across the fields
with him. An early sun
blurs your view of cows,
smudges tops of trees.
Talk is easy between you.
You try your hand at writing.
You write about butterflies
and an old man, he of doorways.
His poems are good, considering;
yours are better, but then
you've had more practice.

Come and paint trees with me,
he says and you climb into
the afternoon. Woods breathe
shadows and smell of peat.
He draws with charcoal.
His trees are strong, full
of summer vigour. Afterwards
he fills a wall with trees,
painting colour over colour,
line upon line. Not bad,
he says of your one tree.
What you need is practice.

You sit together in the bar
stroll into the sweet dark.
I've got red wine at my place.
Like to come? he says and you say
Why not? You sit on the bed
drinking from thick tumblers.
You look at his paintings.
He listens to your poems.

You admire his velvet jacket.
He says he likes your dress,
its soft texture, the way it folds
about you. Much later
the jacket and the Indian print
are the least of your concerns.
The loving is articulate,
full of movement and colour.
So it should be, you've both
had lots of practice;
he with his paintings,
you with your poems.

No fool

At her age
she should have
known better, should
have left a bit
of herself high
on a shelf
out of reach.

'Crazy,'
he had said,
scooping up kisses
under the odd
shooting star knowing
he was far enough
from home.

In her mind
she counted off days
storing them, end-on,
took him at his word
opened like a sea
anemone where he
was concerned.

She played it
all wrong, relaxed.
He pocketed the star,
threw her back
in the pool where
she belonged, poor fool,
and was gone.

Letting go

One day
I will cry again.

I'll scatter
childhood photographs
across the floor
and step on them.

I'll write my name
in the dust
on the bookcase
shelf, stare

at my neighbours
from the front
window. I'll eat
chocolate bars

instead of
low-fat yoghurt.
I'll let the dark
of night take over

until I can't see
to read, perhaps
light a candle –
if I can find

a match. I'll chew
over secrets
like tasteless gum,
lie quiet, quiet

in my long skirts.
The smell of
Albertine roses
will intoxicate me.

One morning
I'll wake up
in the bright of day
beside some man

and I swear
I will cry again.

Nothing new under the sun

By that time, spring had run out of steam
for her. We pointed out the tidal waves
of blossom, bluebells, fields where cows
paddled deep in surging buttercups.

She turned her head, but did not see.
'Mr McCracken, Buster's father, you remember?
He won't survive another season,' she said.
'And Mrs Stephenson at number 48 –

wasn't her Jean in your class? – she died
last week.' We stopped the car, wound down
the windows and a hushed green air washed
over us. Young leaves moved and murmured.

'Just listen to the birds,' we said. 'Tea,
I could do with a cup of tea. Anyway,
you know I can't hear birdsong, not with
my deaf old ears.' We drove on home.

She drank her tea, spoke of neighbours
and the price of butter. Tulips stood
battle-bright and tall, and a thousand
small suns lit the Jews' Mallow bush.

'Beautiful?' we asked. 'Like overgrown
dandelions,' she said. Her last spring
bloomed unseen under a hospital window,
but by then it was all old hat to her.

For a great-grandchild it was different,
all new as words; worms, the warm earth,
Mallow flowers. 'Dandle-lions?' he guessed,
their colour making amber of his eyes.

Weekend in Paris

Well, anyone can dream, I suppose.

Couples sat around interlocked, or
swayed together as they strolled
kissing, kissing, their passion
open as flowers in the mid-day sun.
Now and again they paused for breath,
murmured, lips pressed against the
other's ear. They slid sweets into
mouths, shared them at the next kiss.

And they were all so young. Fresh,
beautiful, passionate. Of course,
the setting was just right, the
slow-flowing Seine, the bridges of
Paris, time of day. We bought hot
chestnuts, one bag between us. We
too walked by the river, held hands.
Old we may be, but romantic as they.

Just one thing, age made us invisible.

Men of Mystery

'Black woolly stockings turn me on,'
        he said.
'Long black woolly stockings
        and white ankle socks.'
And this sixty-year-old, unabashed,
looked as he must have done
                        at nineteen or so.

We live with men. We know their
        little ways,
(small change on the dressing table,
        bath towels waterfall-wet
                        morning erections.)
Yet we are always taken by surprise
        when they voice their passions.

Hard to tell what goes on beneath
        the smart grey suit,
                the Old School blazer,
                        the neatly-knotted tie.
Do they dream of schoolgirls
        these balding men,
                the almost-paid-off mortgage
                        in their sights?

We know their outside skins. Our
experienced fingers can route-march
across their bodies blindfold,
        (give or take the odd
                difference in height
                        or build.)

We know the shape and texture
of their most intimate parts
        testicles like kiwi-fruit,
                penis curled into itself
                        like a rose in bud,
                or standing upright
                        tulip-tipped.

We know where they are vulnerable
    in the crook of the elbow,
    in the small of the back,
    on the baby-soft skin where
               toes meet foot.

We are talking walking encyclopaedias
    on men,
yet pig-ignorant at times. They are
the other sex, closed books to us.

I ponder the familiar face, puzzle
    over his thoughts.
I think about black woolly stockings,
    decide against them;
          they're too scratchy,
            I'm too old.

Learning by doing

When my father died
it was for the first time
and neither of us had
any previous experience
to go on, so we had
     to play it by ear.

From the high hospital
window we could see
cemetery crosses spiking
the skyline, all gilded
in late September sun.
     He joked about it.

Nothing original, of
course, but not bad in
the circumstances. My car
had broken down. 'Borrow
mine – for now,' he said,
     emphasising now.

We both knew it was
a gift for good. 'Get
me some white lemonade,
please love.' He kept it
all low-key, undramatic.
     Then he slept.

I sat by him dry-eyed.
'Don't die, Dad. Please
don't die,' I whispered.
'I'm doing my best not to,'
he said, looking just himself
     in yellow pyjamas.

Given a second chance
we might do it all
differently, make longer
speeches, say 'Good-bye'.
I'd give us a C-, next time,
     MUST TRY HARDER.